10 9 8 7 6 5 4 3 2 1

Copyright© 2024 by CHEETAH® Toys & More, LLC.

No part of this publication may be reproduced, distributed, or transmitted in any form or by any means, including photocopying, recording, or other electronic or mechanical methods, without the prior written permission of the publisher, except in the case of brief quotations embodied in critical reviews and certain other non-commercial uses permitted by copyright law.

ISBN 13: 978-1-964243-61-0
ISBN 10: 1-964243-61-0

Permission request(s) should be submitted to the publisher in writing at one of the addresses below:
CHEETAH® Toys & More, LLC
207 Main Street, 3rd Floor
Hartford, CT 06106 USA

Port Antonio PO
Portland, Jamaica

info@mycheetahinc.com
paulettetrowers@yahoo.com
WhatsApp: 860-781-1726, 876-909-6311

My Own Jamaican Foods From Plants

Aa

ackee

I can write! I can draw!

_____

....

_____

Aa

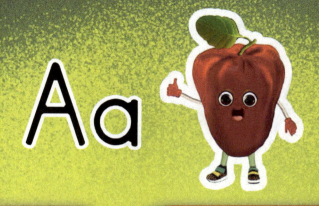

apple

I can write! I can draw!

_____

....

_____

Aa

Avocado

I can write! I can draw!

_____

_____

_____

Bb

breadfruit

I can write! I can draw!

_____

· · · · · · · · · · · · · · · · · · ·

_____

Cc

calalloo

I can write! I can draw!

_____

_____

_____

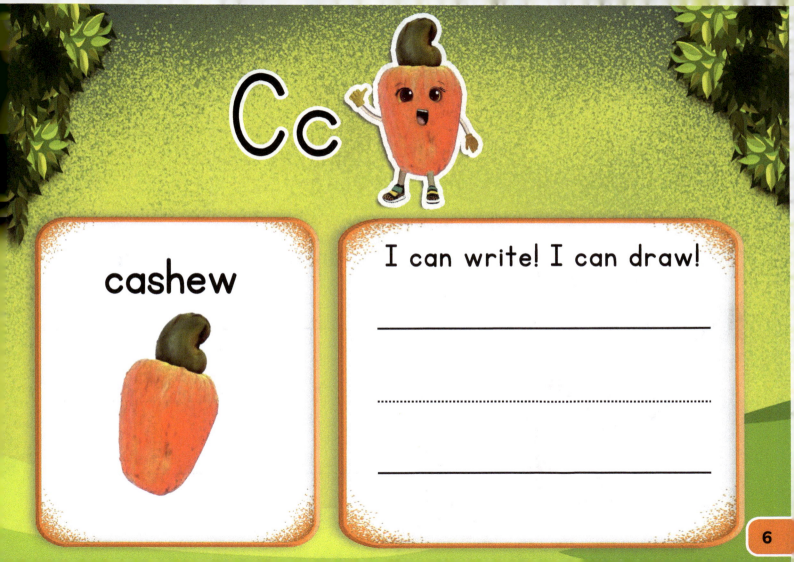

Cc

cashew

I can write! I can draw!

Cc

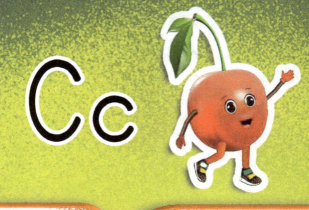

cherry

I can write! I can draw!

_____

....

_____

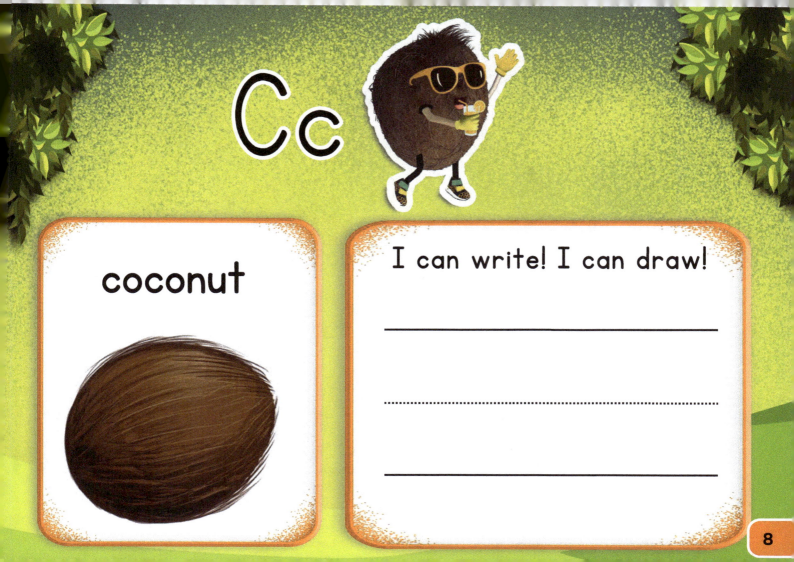

Gg

grapefruit

I can write! I can draw!

_____

_____

_____

Gg

guava

I can write! I can draw!

10

Gg

guinep

I can write! I can draw!

_____

_____

_____

Gg

Gungo pea

I can write! I can draw!

_____

_____

_____

Jj

jackfruit

I can write! I can draw!

_____

_____

_____

Mm

mango

I can write! I can draw!

_____

_____

16

Nn

naseberry

I can write! I can draw!

_____

_____

_____

Oo

orange

I can write! I can draw!

_____

_____

_____

P p

pepper

I can write! I can draw!

_____

. . . .

_____

P p

pineaple

I can write! I can draw!

_____

_____

Pp

plum

I can write! I can draw!

_____

_____

_____

Pp

pumpkin

I can write! I can draw!

_____

....

_____

22

Ss

soursop

I can write! I can draw!

_____

_____

_____

Ss

sweetsop

I can write! I can draw!

_____

_____

_____

Tt

tamarind

I can write! I can draw!

25

Tt

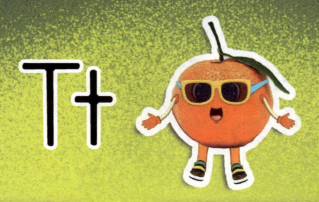

tangerine

I can write! I can draw!

_____

_____

_____

Ss

starfruit

I can write! I can draw!

_____

_____

_____

27

Ss

sugar cane

I can write! I can draw!

_____

- - - - - - - - - - -

_____

Printed in the USA
CPSIA information can be obtained
at www.ICGtesting.com
LVHW082057011124
795478LV00040B/309